Girl,
I See You

Girl, I See You
Conversations Women Need to Have

Tojuan W. Minus

TBLAZEN
MINISTRIES

Girl, I See You: Conversations Women Need to Have
Copyright © 2023 by Tojuan W. Minus

ISBN: 979-8-9879981-1-3

Published by: Tblazen LLC.
Printed in the United States of America

Author Photos:
Internal Layout and Design: InSCRIBEd Inspiration, LLC.
Edited by: Donald Minus, Tojuan Minus, Renita Quick,
         Tonie Smarr

Cover Art: Trinity Minus with Penda L. James

Cover Image: iStock-1386889753 is used under license from stock.adobe.com.

All real-life anecdotes are told with permission from actual parties involved and recorded to the best of the author's recollection. Names in some instances have not been used at the request of the individuals referenced. In some cases, parties mentioned are deceased. Details of some instances have been slightly modified to enhance readability, or to ensure privacy. Any resemblance of any other parties is purely coincidental.

All rights reserved. No part of this book may be reproduced or transmitted in any form electronic, or mechanical, including photocopying and recording, or held in any information storage and retrieval system without permission in writing from the author and publisher.

FOREWORD

As the Director & Founder of The Diamonds Program, a Mentoring and Enrichment Program for girls ages 10-18, it is my passion and purpose to empower women and girls so that they may reach their fullest potential and achieve true success. When I was asked to write the Foreword for this book I was honored to do so.

From the moment I met Tojuan, I could see that she is a woman on a mission to make a difference—a true trailblazer. Tojuan and her husband are members of our church family, Exodus Evangelical Ministries, Inc. in Englewood, Ohio. I find her to be a woman of faith, love, and integrity. She reaches out with such love to assist women and children, wanting only the best for everyone that crosses her path.

As you read this book, you are going to discover that the author's life experiences of hard knocks, disappointments, mistakes made, and perseverance served to make her the woman she is today. Whatever you have had to endure in this life, just know that someone else has been where you are. In this book, Tojuan is unapologetically transparent.

If you've been thinking about what to do with your shame and wondering if you will ever heal from your pain, I believe that *"Girl I See You!"* will be a great source of hope, inspiration, and encouragement to you.

Girl, your life is not over. Girl, you are stronger than you think. We all have things that we would do differently if we could. Girl, I see in you potential and purpose. Girl! God sees you and He loves you. He always has and He always will. May you move forward now and be blessed.

Pamela Maddox, Co-Pastor,
Exodus Evangelical Ministries, Inc., CEO
The Kept Women of God Conferences, Founder

ACKNOWLEDGEMENTS

To **God Be the Glory** for the Things He has done.

I would be remiss if I did not thank those of you who are part of my **Unpluckable Faith Community**. You served as my accountability team, the wind beneath my wings and the sounding board for all things pertaining to *Girl, I See You!* Without your strength, encouragement, rebukes and charges, this work would not have come into fruition. Thank you for saying, "Yes, we will journey with you Tojuan."

To my **Mother**, a pillar of strength. I love you and thank you.

Donald, my Lover, my Friend, my cut-up partner, my sounding board, the "writing style police" thank you for covering me.

Kevin, my only begotten son. You challenge me to be more. **Courtney**, my daughter in love, thank for loving my Kevin.

Kimberly, the daughter I prayed for. Thank you for encouraging me and keeping me on track and telling me to get off Facebook and write.

Trinity, the daughter God gave me at the perfect time. My life is richer because you. Thank you for your willingness to help me.

Chari, You challenge me to be more. Thank you for asking me the question on Tuesdays, "Did you write yesterday?" ☺

Renita, my sister, my friend…you are my rock. Thank you for always having my back.

Tonie, my ride or die for life. Those midnight text messages pushed me to the end of this project.

Penda, Scribe Coach extraordinaire. You challenged me and inspired me all the way. You told me to breathe and then write.

Loretta, highly respected woman of God. I love your transparency. Thank you for praying for me, periodt!

Bishop Maddox and Co-Pastor Maddox, you have undergirded my family with prayer and encouraged me every step of the way. Thank you for acknowledging my gifts and creating spaces for me to exercise them at Exodus Ministries.

To **everyone** who was a part of my journey to becoming, I salute and thank you for helping me to understand my purpose and destiny. I See You because I see me.

Table of Contents

Introduction - Girl, I See You xi

Girl, Who Are You? 1
   Girl, I See Your Greatness 3
   Girl, That Ain't You! 17
   Girl, Family Matters 33

Girl, What Do You Need? 51
   Girl, Don't Get Stuck 53
   Girl, Forgive to Heal 61
   Girl…Breathe! 71
   Girl, Trust in the Truth 79
   Girl, Who Is In Your Tribe? 83

Girl, What IS Love? 93
   Girl, Sex Is A Gift 95
   Girl, Is Marriage For You? 103

Conclusion 121
   Girl, You are Strong 122

INTRODUCTION - GIRL, I SEE YOU

When I was growing up, we didn't have certain conversations. Nobody talked about purpose, how to handle people who get on your nerves, sex, marriage, or unplanned pregnancies. Some of it caused unnecessary pain and confusion because I didn't know what I didn't know. I vowed when I became a mature adult to teach my children, sister friends, and other women what I didn't learn so that they would not experience the pain that wisdom could have prevented. Like me, I know that you are on a journey to become whole, value your worth, and understand your greatness.

This book is my gift to you. I am going to be real with you. I will not let the shame from my past prevent me from being authentic. You need the whole truth so that you can walk in wholeness and peace in every aspect of your life. How can you glean from a leader if she doesn't come all the way clean?

I want you to thrive in every area of your life and to walk in your name, "Victory." You need someone to acknowledge you as the jewel that you are. I want to do that, and this book will help you understand that it is possible to press past your mistakes and shine bright. We all have struggled with something: identity issues, daddy issues, relationships and finding balance. For these reasons, I want to offer hope from my story. You will read about some of my challenges, insights, trip-ups, and ah-ha's.

I have watched women share their stories at church, work, and in the community. In the moment they talk about their fears and shame, but they mask the whole truth. They can make you feel like something is missing in you because you don't have victory in certain areas or situations. They lead you to believe that their life is peaches and cream when it's not. I am willing to open my heart and share my struggles so that you know that you are not alone.

While you are reading I want you to feel like we are sitting together having a conversation. I use the word "Girl" as a term of endearment and when I use the word, it means that we are connecting on a personal, emotional, and spiritual level.

Words are like power surges in the atmosphere. They can elevate, deflate, encourage, or tear down. Sticks and stones break your bones AND words can hurt you if you are not settled in your identity. When I say, "Girl I See You," I mean it.

"I use the word "Girl," affectionately.

For me, it means that we are connecting on a personal, emotional, and spiritual level."

How To Use This Book

Girl, I See You will teach you how to look deep into yourself and not be repelled by what you see. This is important to me because I want you to fulfill your purpose in life.

I want you to know that there is a Lover of your soul that embraces all of you; good, bad, ugly, your struggles, pain, and hope. I know you may not read the Bible regularly, so I have given you examples of people in the Bible to show that what you are going through is not new.

1. Go to your secret place with your coffee or tea and get lost in this book.
2. Spend time getting to know yourself.
3. Read the scriptures in different versions.
4. Reflect on the questions.
5. Find a sister, friend, or group where you can discuss the topics in a non-judgmental environment.
6. Share this book with others.

Girl, I loosened my shackles and opened my heart so that it would give you the courage and confidence to do the same.

Tojuan

Girl, I See You

Girl, I've been seeing you all over town.
Walking around with your head down.
Like a badge, you are wearing a frown.
I see you sitting across from me in the office.
I see you in meetings with the forced smile, masking what is really inside.
You are in the grocery store!
You are in the laundromat.
I see you at the bus stop.
I see you rushing into the day care to avoid late fees.
I see that you are tired.
I SEE YOU!
I see me in you.
Day in and day out you hustle wondering if there is more to this life than what you are experiencing.
Girl, there is more for you because Girl, I see you.
I see beyond the obvious.
When I see you, I see purpose and destiny before me.
Do you see it?

Girl, WHO ARE YOU?

GIRL, I SEE YOUR GREATNESS

Elkannah, Hannah, and Peninnah
1 Samuel 1:1-27

There was a man named Elkannah who had two wives, Hannah and Peninnah. Girl let's pause right here. Having more than one wife during biblical times was allowed for several reasons. It was a patriarchal society. In other words, men were the leaders and providers. Most women did not have an education and were unskilled laborers. They did not have the ability to take care of themselves. They could not just go apply for a job and get their own "paper," their own place to stay, their own car or buy their own designer looks.

Unmarried women back then needed provisions and protection. They couldn't just make it happen. Male relatives like fathers, brothers, cousins, and uncles provided basic necessities: food, shelter, clothing, safety, and protection for women. Although this was not ideal, or God's best plan for marriage, many women were in this situation. The alternatives for unmarried women were prostitution or slavery and possibly starvation. Because of this dynamic, some men had several wives. Of course, having many wives created a competitive vibe for the women.

Peniiiiiiinnah!

Girl, let me tell you, if you don't encounter a Peninnah in your life, I will boldly say you are not growing and you are stagnant. Into every life a Peninnah will come. She will pick on you or she will push you towards your greatness. Most times both things are happening at the same time.

Some people thrive on making others feel less than them. They look down on you. In their mind they think they have arrived at a status that they think you will never apprehend.

I have learned that when people see the greatness in you it can either be that they are jealous of you and want to hold you down, or they want to push you into your destiny. In my life this has been true in relationships with several people.

My Work Experience

I was the Director of an Early Learning Center and needed a Preschool Teacher for the evening shift. A teacher on my staff recommended her friend LovelyJoy. She applied and at our interview I couldn't help but smile when I saw her. Her smile was infectious. She made me want to smile. She was a pretty girl and full of jubilant life. She was like a fresh breeze of joy. I saw her in the beginning of her becoming and it was phenomenal. Her light was bright.

I knew I would hire her instantly and was just going through the formalities. LovelyJoy was different, a rare jewel. Her light was always shining bright. She was energizing. The children loved her, and she was always fully engaging with them. She was the big sister that would play with them continuously. Her stamina was non-stop. As a teacher, she was a natural, a gift to the early childhood education field.

LovelyJoy

I loved working with LovelyJoy. We had mutual respect for each other. Her greatness was evident. Whenever I sent her to a training or workshop, she would return and talk about the different organizations trying to recruit her to work with them. She would say, "I'm not leaving you, Mrs. Minus. I like working with you."

The feeling was mutual. I was not intimidated by LovelyJoy's reports. In fact, I celebrated them. LovelyJoy was dynamic and her greatness could not be deflated.

LovelyJoy asked to meet with me to discuss her future. She wanted to pursue a master's degree in education. Our organization would only offer her limited resources in terms of scholarship. LovelyJoy was a single mother, and it would require her to navigate through many obstacles to continue her education, but I knew of a sure way she could do it.

At our meeting, I shared how I knew she could get her master's degree for free. I knew if she went to work at this other early childhood education center at the local university, continuing education was required as part of the performance evaluation of the teaching positions. She would be able to take courses for free at the university.

I told her, "I care about you as a person. It would be selfish of me to want you to stay here. Our programs would not offer you the opportunity to advance like the university. Here, you would be paying for most of your tuition out of pocket. At the university, your tuition would be free."

She was shocked and said, "You want me to leave?" I told her I did not want her to leave, but that working at the university would help her reach her goal of obtaining a master's degree without the burden of paying college tuition. Most of the early childhood education teachers had masters degrees. Taking courses contributed to high performance evaluations and salary increases at the university.

Truly, I did not want her to leave, but I counseled her not from my selfish desires. I wanted her to soar and fulfill her goals and dreams. Maybe it was my mothering nature, but in my mind, I was saying "fly butterfly fly!" LovelyJoy did not leave our organization. I ended up leaving before LovelyJoy. She became the Assistant Director and maintained that position until the center closed. We stayed connected through social media. Years later she reached out to me to share about getting her master's degree and she was opening her own Early Learning Center.

I believe that as sisters in leadership, we need to love and support each other. We should not try to hold people in positions that benefit us. That's selfish. We need to look and see what the best thing for them is and push them towards it, even if that means they're not physically with you.

Even though I knew she was one of the most dynamic preschool teachers I had met, I knew that she needed to go to grow. I was provoking LovelyJoy to her purpose, not to irritate her, but to stir up her gifts.

My Church Experience

If you watch those reality shows and you know the ones I am talking about, you have watched the "Peninnahs" provoke the "Hannahs". Peninnah and Hannah are both beautiful, but Peninnah lets Hannah know, "I still have something you don't have. " Hannah and Peninnah eventually have a big fight. The spectacle of the scene is predictable and happens over and over again on those shows. Girl, sometimes the catalyst to your greatness is the one that gets on your nerves.

Most of my Peninnah encounters occurred in the church. You see, there is this image that church women have it all together. The church is the arena where for the most part, the women are celebrated. However, there are some who have it together and others are in process.

My naïveté got me into a lot of situations in church. I was a natural leader, but at times I was head strong. In my season of awakening and starting to understand my giftings, my Peninnah's were quick to let me know what I did not possess and what box they wanted me to stay in. A Peninnah will usually see your greatness and will be jealous or intimidated by it, especially if Peninnah is used to being the center of attention.

In innocence, I poked some bears so to speak. I bumped into a couple of people that were just as head strong as me, but because of their positions and influence I always ended up on the short end of the stick. Baby, when those Peninnah's came after me, it was no joke. I would usually go somewhere and lick my wounds and try again.

There were people who saw the potential of my giftings and what I could become in church leadership and tried to squash it. While others were seeing the value of my giftings and encouraged me. Girl, time has taught me to recognize these scenarios and try to be a positive influence in these situations.

Dr. Cee

I first encountered Dr. Cee at a women's conference I attended many years ago. I was sitting in the front row because I was assisting the guest worship leader. Dr. Cee was the teacher for the workshop. After teaching on "Identification Intercessory Prayer," which is finding hinderances that are affecting the atmosphere and people in a region. The Bible calls it dealing with principalities and powers and identifying the strongman controlling certain areas.

Dr. Cee started praying for people in the class, which was normal in my church environment. She walked towards me, and I thought, "Uh Oh!" She picked up and removed my Bible from my lap and sat it on a chair next to me. She stood me up. I bowed my head and closed my eyes and with my hands lifted in surrender, I waited for her to say something to me.

Several minutes later, I could feel ushers trying to lift me off the floor. My friends told me, Dr. Cee touched my stomach, and I waved bye-bye and hit the floor. LOL! We called that being slain in the spirit or falling under the power of God, although for me it was more like a knockout. She never said anything to me. I didn't say anything to her. Because I understood about laying on of hands, I knew there was a spiritual release from her to me as it relates to Identification Intercessory Prayer.

The next year at the women's conference, Dr. Cee was a speaker again. Girl, I had learned from the year before and I sat in the last row in the middle of the row at the workshop. She finished her teaching on prayer and once again started praying for people. I felt secure on the back row until she started walking down the aisle towards the back row. Aww man, not again. She came to the back row and scooted past the other women and grabbed my hand.

I sat my Bible down just in time on a chair. Once again, I hit the floor. In my mind I was like, "God, you are funny."

Dr. Cee is a powerful pray-er. She walks in such power and authority as it relates to spiritual matters, especially evangelism of cities. Years later, I developed an evangelism template called The City Gates Project that brought people from different backgrounds together for one purpose, to share the love of God to all in our city, one house, one block, one community at a time. One day I was walking downtown in my city and praying for the issues that were plaguing our city. It was at that moment; I knew why she prayed for me all those years ago. She saw something in me that I had not seen in myself. She saw the potential of me doing exactly what I was doing.

If she had told me what she saw all those years prior, I would have rejected it, out of fear. So, she imparted strength and courage to me. Her teachings led to me study the history of my city, names of streets, certain neighborhoods, and the political history. This study would equip me to pray in a way that my prayers would effect change in the spiritual climate as well as the natural climate. Her teaching was the foundation on which I learned about Identification Intercessory Prayer.

Back to Peninnah and Hannah...

One of the most wonderful gifts God gave people was sexual intercourse. This act of intimacy was gifted to husbands and wives for basically three reasons: procreation, relaxation, and recreation. Procreation or having children was major and women who produced children were honored. Barren women were looked upon with shame and contempt. The scripture says Peninnah had sons and daughters. So Peninnah had at least four children. Peninnah was productive and the evidence was children. Hannah had nothing to show for her efforts. Peninnah and her children were a reminder to Hannah that she was a non-producer.

How to Understand Your Greatness

Hannah had to have a talk with God to understand her greatness and to become productive. She wanted to produce something of her own. Hannah's infertility was more than physical. Her purpose and destiny were infertile and impotent as well. Hannah's life was predictable. She was going through the motions every year doing the same ritual. They went to a certain city to worship God and Elkanah would give Hannah double offering to put before God. Peninnah would provoke Hannah because in addition to Elkanah's offerings, she had children.

Lack of purpose and focus will have you doing things for no clear reason…wandering aimlessly, going through the motions, confused, no goals, stuck in your familiar, existing.

Hannah wanted more for herself. Elkanah could not calm Hannah's heart and help her to be content with being a non-producer because Elkanah did not fully understand Hannah's purpose and destiny. Elkanah was like, "Woman, I love YOU! You are so focused on Peninnah, and I am supplying for you better than her."

Hannah could not embrace his love for her completely because she felt something was missing in her. Lack of children caused Hannah to feel worthless. She complained to Elkanah about this. I can hear the complaining and comparing herself to Peninnah. She was blaming Elkanah. She made the situation about others by saying things like, "Peninnah is mean to me."

Elkanah could not give Hannah her heart's desire because her purpose and destiny originated with God. Hannah had to connect with her Creator. He was the One she needed to confront so that she could be productive. Hannah knew deep inside she was not created to be a non-producer.

Girl, there's a part of us that no one can fully understand. It's like when an artist paints a masterpiece. Others can look at it and they can study it and give their interpretation of what they think it is all about. But they really don't know what it is all about. It is the creator of the masterpiece that fully understands why strokes of paint were placed in a certain way. You are God's masterpiece. He created you for a specific reason, a purpose. It has been said there are two important days in a person's life. The first is the day you are born. The second is when you discover why you were born. Girl, that's your purpose. Usually, your purpose is beneficial to others around you or in your community. Girl, live your life with purpose in mind.

GIRL, THAT AIN'T YOU!

Simon, Peter, and Jesus
Matthew 16:13-22

When Simon first encounters Jesus, Simon is fishing with his brother Andrew. Jesus passes by and says, "Follow Me and I will make you fishers of men." Basically, Jesus said quit this job and come with me, because this is not the best for you. Lay down the familiar identity of yourself and follow Me. Jesus said, "Come "and they came. Jesus is still saying the same thing today, "Follow Me!"

Think about it, when God calls us, He has something better for us to do. It takes courage to stop being or doing what you always done and journey to the new.

There are many lessons to learn from this passage of scripture. The beauty of the Bible is it is always unveiling deeper and deeper truths. You can read the same scriptures for 20 years and then in year 21 you see it in a completely different light. A lot of times it is when you are ready for the deeper truths of the Word of God.

Girl, you want people in your life that challenge you to be your genuine self. I have a person in my life I call Teacher who taught me many things. He helped me to understand the power of prayer and he taught me how to pray God's word. In a time in my life when I did not fully understand who I was, he made some hard truths clear to me.

Teacher

Some of my earlier encounters with Teacher were in passing. He had come from Nigeria, and he was attending my church. I would greet him as I was passing him in the hall. I begin to notice how he stared at people. He had an intensity about him. I thought it was odd at first. Because of his strong accent, when he spoke, I had to really listen to what he was saying. Of course, I would repeat what I thought he was saying. He would then correct me by saying something else. We went back and forth like that for a while until my ears were trained to understand his words despite the accent.

As I got to know him, I found him to be wise. He spoke to me with stories. The bible calls them parables. A parable is a story to teach a truth. In other words, it will tell you something, without exactly telling you. It was for you to figure out the parable. Parables make you think beyond the obvious. Teacher spoke in parables often.

You see once I recognized his wisdom and the depth of his knowledge of spiritual things, I wanted discipling.

Disciples are followers of Christ. I wanted Teacher to share his knowledge on how I could grasp the richness of the Bible and follow Jesus on a deeper level. I wanted my prayers to carry power and not just be empty ramblings. Many people just read the Bible like a textbook in school. A person highlights what the teacher talked about in class and remembers it for the tests. At least, that was my approach in some classes. But I wanted a deeper understanding of the mysteries and truths in the Bible.

I remember the day I got up the nerve to ask him to disciple me. I took a friend with me for reinforcement and encouragement. Teacher was walking down the hall in the church. His cadence was slow and methodical. He walked like a hunched back and slow like he had seen many things in the world and was not impressed by much. With each lifting of his foot, from left to right, he stepped liked his feet hurt, yet his face did not exhibit pain or discomfort. It was almost as if he was looking for someone or something to motivate his strides to increase. I was a little wobbly as I approached him. My friend and I had customary pleasantries with

Teacher, and I just blurted out, "I think you are to disciple me." Without missing a beat in his stride, he kept walking in his hunched pace. He said, "You really think so?" My friend and I chimed in and said yes. He mumbled something like Hmm and just kept walking. We stopped and watched him continue to walk down the hall. I knew he had answered me. I knew he agreed to disciple me because his stride had changed a little.

He reminded me of Yoda from Star Wars in stature, wit, and wisdom. He was like Mr. Miyagi, and I was the awkward unrefined Karate Kid. He was unconventional in his approach. Like the Karate Kid, I would have to learn "to wax on and wax off" in a certain way.

When I saw him at church, he would share parables. I would leave his presence confused and dumbfounded sometimes, yet I was a sponge that wanted more of his wisdom. Teacher is not the only person that I gleaned from during that season in my life, but he was in the forefront.

I remember our church having what we call all night prayer. We would gather in the church and pray from 9pm to 6am. I remember Teacher chiding those who brought pillows and blankets.

He wanted to know if we were coming to pray or have a slumber party. Some people were offended by his comments, but I thought it was funny. I still laugh about it to this day. If he stood for hours and prayed, I stood as well. If he sat, I sat. He never told me to do that, I did it on my own. It taught me discipline. He taught me how to pray with authority and power.

The day came when he said something to me that wasn't in a parable. I was striving with several people at church. We were not seeing eye to eye, and I was really frustrated by it all. Of course, I felt I was right. In my mind, these people, because of their higher position in church were just being mean for no reason.

I had been telling people that I was a sweet little angel, a cherub. My friends would chuckle whenever I said it. You see that is how I wanted people to perceive me. Everybody liked cherubs. I wanted to be liked by everyone because I was teased a lot as a child and wanted to fit in. I was not bothering anyone, so I did not understand why I was getting all this clapback from certain people.

I had a volatile meeting at church one evening and as I was leaving, I saw Teacher. I shared with him what happened. I was looking for sympathy. I was looking for someone to confirm my point of view. I wanted him to say I was right.

Girl, Teacher got in my face. I was confused. In my mind I was already in fight mode. The sweet cherub wanted to fight. In my mind, Teacher was very close to me…too close. My fine mustache hair started to singe. He said, "You do not know what happens in the spirit when you walk in a room."

Totally confused, I said, "I don't bother anyone. Anyone can say anything to me. I am a cherub." (Cherubs are loved and don't fight…right???) I wanted to really give those people a piece of my mind. I had had enough of them.

He said, "They wouldn't dare get in your face and say the things I say." He emphasized; "they wouldn't dare." Teacher continued, "I don't have anything to lose so I don't care. I will say what I have to say even if you never speak to me again."

Teacher stepped close to me, and I could feel his frustration with my self-pity. He said, "Your perception of yourself is fake." I remember him saying, "Your problem is you don't know who you are."

I felt my lips quiver and I stared at him in bewilderment. He looked me straight in the eyes and said, "Go somewhere and figure out who you are."

The inferno of those words left me stunned. Not only were my mustache hairs singed, but the ignition of his words also sparked something in my soul. Like the opening scene of the old Mission Impossible television show, he lit a match, started a fire, and left me to process the weight of his words. I watched him turn away from me in that hunched stride and walked away just as I was opening my mouth to respond. I was stupefied by his abrupt rudeness, yet I was intrigued all at the same time.

His words pierced my existence. Go somewhere and figure out who you are kept ringing over and over in my head. I thought I knew who I was. It was a defining moment in my life. My focus quickly shifted from why this person was picking on me to what she saw in me that made her "come after me" all the time.

I asked myself, "Who am I to her? What am I provoking in her? What name is defining me to her? Who am I to myself? What name am I using to define myself? What am I saying about myself in my mind?"

Lack of knowing self can create problems in our lives. My self-esteem was low. It was clear when I kept referring to myself as a sweet cherub. I wanted to be liked by everyone.

As a child, I was suspended from school twice. Once in elementary and once in junior high. So, if I was going to be honest, I knew there was a stubbornness in me. I wanted to be perceived as a cherub (fake), sweet, innocent, and liked by all when in reality I was more like a warring angel willing to go into battles. This fluctuation between the fake image I thought would make people like me and the reality of who I was created to be caused an unbalanced and unhealthy sense of self. Part of me wanted to please people because I wanted them to like me and the other part of me wanted to tell people to go kick rocks. I was schizophrenic in my identity of self.

My perception of myself was warped. Perceptions are real, but not necessarily true. However, perceptions can override TRUTH. The truth was I did not want to really embrace the me that God created me to be. Truth is, I can walk in a room, and you know I am there even if I don't open my mouth. My presence is felt. My personality can be larger than life, yet deep inside this warring angel is a gentle child of God whose heart is tender towards the things of God.

As I accepted the challenge from Teacher, I went on a journey of self-discovery. I realized that others had named me according to their perceptions. I have been many things to many people: smart (really a life-long learner), shy (until, you know me), quiet (sometimes), bossy(don't like the term), funny (it's necessary), servant, leader , difficult (hmm), hard-headed(sometimes), team player, strong, passionate, controlling, cry baby (yep, according to my children), fat & Black (yes and yes) , nigger (many Black people have been called this by white people) wild horse, mountain goat, velvet hammer and a b@tch!

I embrace some of these definitions of me, others I had to learn to reject. In my mind I have had to say, "Girl, that ain't you."

When I was growing up if any one called me the B word, it was grounds for a fight. It was an insult against everything feminine. There are many foundational definitions for this word:

- a female dog in heat,
- a difficult malicious, mean woman;

- a submissive subservient slave (remember when Beyonce said, "Bow down B-tches!");
- a prostitute or whore.

There has been an evolutionary journey of this word. It was once a word that was despised, but now it is a term of endearment. Many women use this word to mean a strong, no nonsense boss chick who is in charge of her sexuality. Our feminist forward society has weaponized this word to describe a woman as "powerful and strong." They want you to wear this word as a badge of honor, a symbol of nobility and status, but I want you to consider what God says about you. He calls you:

- Beloved
- Apple of His eye
- Daughter
- More than a conqueror
- Victory

When someone calls you out of your name, say to yourself, "Girl, that ain't you." That will help you remember to eat the meat and spit out the bones. Perceptions are real but not necessarily truth. Say that to yourself, too.
Sometimes people are assessing you through their life experiences. If you say or do something

that reminds someone of a good experience in their life you can be perceived in a positive light. Girl, if you remind them of a painful memory, watch out. You will probably never do anything good in that person's opinion.

Have you heard people say, "she acts just like such and such." Or "She reminds me of my mean Auntie. She frowns and fusses like my strict grandmother used to. God rest her soul. "

I even had someone say that she gets a funny feeling when she is around me. (Really, is it me or do you need to heal?)

Back to Simon, Peter, and Jesus

Simon and his brother Andrew were journeying with Jesus all around their local community. They were part of His crew of 12. The 12 were the disciples that were always with Him. Word got out about all the miracles Jesus was performing and crowds would gather to see what was going on. They were chilling one day, and Jesus asked the disciples, "What are the people saying about who I am?"
The disciples answered and said they are saying, "You remind them of some historic people of the past."

Jesus then asked His disciples, those close to Him, "Who do you think I am?" After all, the disciples had been traveling with Him for 3 years. They had to have formed opinions about Jesus.

Simon, answered and said, "You are the Christ, the Son of the Living God." Jesus said to Simon that he was correct, and that people didn't tell him that, but His heavenly Father revealed Jesus true identity to Simon. Jesus said Simon, "You shall now be called Peter and upon this rock (truth, strong foundation) I will build my church."

When we are ready for deeper truth there is a shift in our identity. Our nature changes. In the Bible, we see it as name changes. People through-out scripture are redefined by God. When they tap into their real purpose, God renames them. The real you will show up when you tap into a deeper knowledge and understanding of God.

People are going to describe you with many adjectives, nouns, and exclamation points. It's what you respond to internally that determines your identity. The Bible says as a (hu)man thinks so is he. If your inner talk agrees with the descriptive narrative of others, you will react to the narrative. Remember in the Color Purple when Mister said nothing would ever come of Celie? He called her Black, poor, ugly, a woman, nothing at all!!!

Celie's response was she is poor, Black, and maybe even ugly, but she was here. She acknowledged the obvious, but she would no longer let him define her worth. She said I am here. Girl, you are here, and you matter. How you see yourself matters. We are all in process and working on something. Don't let what others think about you be the final say when you are transitioning to your greater self. God wants you to see yourself as He sees you. Acknowledge where you have been and what you have done but keep growing and going in God.

I remember Arsenio Hall interviewing Whoopie Goldberg and he said she was fine. She struggled to accept it. Perhaps, Whoopie was used to people calling her funny, not fine. I know that feeling well. It was hard for her to accept the compliment. Been there done that. Listen to negative descriptions about yourself long enough and you will believe the negative comments.

I believe Whoopie had been trained by the world's definition of beauty: thin, blond, and blue eyes. She was conditioned to see her beauty as ugly. Funny thing was, I saw the beauty he was seeing in that moment. Her skin was glowing. She had a big hair don't care wig on. Her make-up was minimal. She doesn't need a lot. She did not have on any glasses. Her eyes sparkled. She looked good. Let's normalize telling people when they look good. But first, say it to yourself. Say, I look good.

During my season of discovery when I was trying to figure out who I was for real, I was called a mountain goat. An outside observer was watching what I was dealing with at church, approached me and said she felt sorry for me and my family. I told her don't you dare feel sorry for me (growth). God allowed me to be in this situation. I did not want pity, I wanted to understand what was happening in my world. My response caused her to say I reminded her of a mountain goat. In my Gary Coleman voice I was like, "Whatcha talking about, Willis?"

She explained that mountain goats have special hooves to help them grip the side of mountains. They can literally walk sideways on mountains and not lose their grip. You are showing that kind of strength. When problems come, you don't crumble, you stand strong. The mountain of challenges will not overtake you; you will walk sideways on the mountain. WOW! WOW! WOW!

I embraced being called a mountain goat. Years later, while visiting Mount Rushmore, while the faces chiseled in the mountain were impressive, I really wanted to see some mountain goats. I affectionally refer to mountain goats as my "peeps."

Teacher challenged me to go somewhere and figure out who I was. I went somewhere and did that. I went in my prayer room and talked about it to the One who made me. Knowing who you are internally is powerful. My identity is found in Christ. I know what happens in the spirit when I come in a room. The genuine me comes in the room.

GIRL, FAMILY MATTERS

The book of the genealogy of Jesus Christ, the Son of David, the Son of Abraham:
Matthew 1:1-18

I have heard people say that there are some nuts in every family tree. I believe this is true. There is no perfect family. Jesus had plenty of drama and characters coming through the family line. There were murderers, thieves, drunks, adulterers, and a whore to name a few. These people served as a reminder to us that it matters where you come from, but it doesn't matter.

Your upbringing doesn't necessarily determine your outcome in life. Yes, it plays a major role in building your initial foundation in life. Some of us had what the world defines as a stable upbringing with two parents loving each other and their children. Some of us were reared in environments considered fragmented: single parent homes with latch key kids. I was a product of the latter.

My mother's factory job making Log Cabin Syrup and Tang required her to leave home before I woke up for school. My alarm clock on school mornings was Momma telephoning the house to tell my brother and me to wake up and get ready for school. Momma usually wasn't back from work when I got home from school. I wore a house key on a chain around my neck. My instructions were clear, go straight home from school, use your key to let yourself in, then latch or lock the door behind you. Do not answer the door if anyone knocks and definitely no friends were allowed to come over until Momma got home. Momma would come home tired with a putrid, sweet scent of syrup and Tang permeating her polyester pants and shirt.

Family foundational environments can shape you and or shake you. This is why two children can live in the same house with the same parent or parents and have different perspectives on their upbringing. Environments can shape how you view your world and the world around you. It could be that all a person knows about life is what she saw growing up. Environments can also shake you up. They can challenge you to look beyond what is familiar. I was reared in an environment that served to shake me and make me look for more that I was accustomed to seeing daily.

The Kitchen Table

Years ago, I took part in a family activity at a conference I attended. The facilitator at the workshop handed everyone a piece of paper. It reminded me of the drawing paper I used in elementary school. He then sat crayons and markers on the table. Our assignment was to draw our kitchen table at dinner time. We were to draw each person in the household at the table. In my mind, I was like this is going to be easy, Momma, Tony, and me.

I drew this brown rectangle. Table done.

He told us to make chairs for each person at the table. Chairs done. Well, they were really more like three lowercase "h's".

He told us to place a name next to each chair. Done.

Next, draw the person. I got this. I am an expert in drawing stick people. I even drew some hair on my stick people.

He then asked us to describe the interaction between the people at the table in any way we wanted on the paper. Some people wrote words, but I drew thought bubbles with pictures above

Momma, Tony, and myself. The facilitator had us get in small groups of five people or so and we had to share what was on our paper.

My heart started beating hard. I thought it was going to come right out of my chest. I didn't know if I really wanted to be transparent with these strangers in my group. I was for sure not going to share first.

One by one people shared. Some in my group had both parents at the table and some didn't. Some had family members just eating, but not interacting with each other. There was no dialog. The family was eating and in their own thoughts. Some people were in the kitchen. Some in other places in the house, not at the table. Some had negative, violent dialog going on between the family members. Some had positive dialog going on. It was my turn to share.

Nervously, I started speaking. Momma was sitting at the head of the table and I at the other end of the table. Tony was sitting on the side with his chair turned away from the table. The picture I drew above Momma was a rain cloud. Momma worked hard to care for Tony and me. Our fathers did not support her financially. We survived paycheck to paycheck. There were many times that the money ran out before the month did. Momma was tired, but she was the only provider for her children. Her dreams were covered by rain clouds. She didn't have time to focus on herself. She loved us because she willingly sacrificed for us.

Tony's chair was turned from the table. I drew scribbles of various colors above his head. His addiction had his mind scrambled, and he was doing his own thing apart from us. Above my head was a rainbow extending from me to my mother.

My rainbow did not cross her rain cloud. I was extending hope to her that things had to get better. Somewhere deep in me, I just knew it had to be more to life than waking up, going to work, paying bills, going to sleep, and getting up and starting it all over again. To be clear, there was plenty of laughter and love in my childhood. Momma would scrape and save money so that we could have some experiences outside of our normal routine.

The "Kitchen Table" exercise served to help the participants get a clearer understanding of how our family dynamic affected our current views about life and relationships. In order for us to reap the benefits of the exercise, it required us to be honest about our familial relationships and how we felt those relationships shaped us.

As a child, I imagined what it would be like to be rich, and Momma did not have to work so hard making Log Cabin Syrup and Tang. Sidebar: To this day, I have not eaten Log Cabin Syrup or drink Tang. Girl, remember we can look back at our past, but we should not get stuck in our past. The Kitchen Table helped me to see that family may look a certain way to an outsider, but the kitchen table may present something different.

Momma's Blues

My mother was one of eleven children. My grandmother had children by different men and by the time my mother was a teenager, she had to care for many of her younger siblings while grandma worked. My grandma married the man who sired her last three children. It was clear that his focus was only on his three children. Momma grew up with dreams of becoming a singer. When she was a teenager, she had an opportunity to compete in a singing contest. She needed a ride to the concert hall where the contest was taking place. My grandma's husband did not think it was important. He wouldn't give her a ride. She missed her opportunity to compete. Girl, some people don't care about your dreams, but keep dreaming.

Momma let her dreams fade as she cleaned house and chased after the young ones. She got pregnant with my brother at nineteen and she had me at twenty-two. She was still living with my grandma during this time. My mother and grandma had a disagreement and grandma said there was only one woman of the house, and it was her. She kicked my momma out of her house.

My momma is resilient. Immediately, she found a place to stay in West Oakland and a place to work. Her neighbor would baby sit me and my brother. The neighbor eventually became her husband. Momma soon discovered her husband was abusive. During this time, she found herself being attracted to a man that she worked with, and she left her husband and she lived with her boyfriend. We all lived in East Oakland at that time.

My momma and her boyfriend lived together from the time I was around four until I was eight years old. Momma's boyfriend had a daughter. Some weekends she would stay with us. When she came over, I took a back seat to her. His focus was only on his daughter, and I was ignored. At least that's how I felt.

Momma's boyfriend had a temper, and he was a womanizer. At that time, Momma worked third shift at the factory. Sometimes, her boyfriend would bring other women over while she was at work. Yes, my brother and I told. One night she got off work early and came home and found another woman asleep in her bed with her man. Baby, reality television had nothing on my mother's street justice. She gently woke up the couple. When they could focus, they could see she was holding her boyfriend's gun.

The screaming and cursing were epic. It ended with momma telling the lady to get out of her house. The lady tried to get her clothes, but momma wasn't having it. The lady went running out of the apartment naked. Momma threatened to kill her boyfriend with his own gun. I could hear all this from my bedroom. Arguing was normal with them. They loved as hard as they fought.

When he would get drunk and become violent, the gun would come out. One time, I heard a loud firecracker sound. He shot the gun during an argument. I was so scared. Later, I learned that he shot a hole in the floor. I stared at that hole a lot when I was in the living room. I thought he could have shot my momma. I am sure my mother thought about it as well. One would wonder why she stayed with him. The reality was she was buying time and saving money so that she could leave. Because he was getting increasingly violent, Momma got in touch with grandma, and we went back to live with her.

By this time grandma and her husband had moved from West Oakland to North Oakland. I wish I could say it was a wonderful time, but I knew grandma's husband did not want us in his house. Momma was able to rent the house right next door to my grandma. I lived in that house until I left home for college.

Daddy Chronicles

God is Jesus' Father
John 14:10

Jesus knew His Daddy was God. Jesus knew that He was accepted and loved by God. However, I have often wondered if children teased Jesus like I was teased as a child. Children would taunt me by singing, "Tojuan, don't have a daddy, to the tune of "Ring Around a Rosie." Children can be cruel someties. I have always had a Daddy.

It has been said that children are nurtured by mommas but pattern their life behaviors after daddies. Daddies teach girls early on how men should value them. But what happens when a daddy isn't present physically and or emotionally? I needed my daddy as a child and I knew him, but he wasn't around. Correction, he was in the same city as me, but for most of my childhood he was not emotionally or physically available for me.

I saw my daddy in snapshots throughout my childhood. I can remember at a certain age I would see him. My daddy would show up unannounced and he would bring gifts and it would be fun and laughter for a couple of days and then he would be gone for years. This pattern of his "some timey" presence in my life made me feel like something was wrong with me, or that I was not important enough to him.

The rejection and his inconsistent presence affected many of my life choices. I looked for affirmation and acceptance in relationships. I was looking for my daddy's love in all the wrong places. I mistook flattering words for love. Some guys knew just what to say to get my attention, but none knew how to capture my heart.

There were times I would cry to my momma, "I want my daddy."

She would respond, "I am your daddy." My momma took care of me and was my provider, I think she felt that I was rejecting her because I wanted to spend time with him. She thought daughters could be fine in life with only their mothers. Afterall, she survived without her father being in her life.

My life work of ministering to women of all backgrounds, ages, and cultures, lets me know that Momma was wrong. Daughters need daddies. Momma needed her daddy, and I needed my daddy as well.

Girl, did you see the pattern? My momma did not have her natural father around. My grandma's husband was not emotionally or physically available for momma. Momma's boyfriend was partially available for me. My daddy wasn't physically or emotionally available for me. This void was rejecting for both my momma and me. Sometimes, to mask the hurt and rejection, women take on the independent mindset. I don't need a man. I got this. Girl, is any of this hitting a nerve in you?

My relationship with my natural father affected how I approached my relationship with my heavenly Father. I expected God to be the same as my natural father. I had trust issues, really abandonment issues. The reality is my daddy abandoned his parental responsibilities to protect, shelter, instruct, care, and support me. I was an orphan in so many ways. Like Orphan Annie, I experienced a hard knock life, but I held on to the notion that the sun would come out tomorrow. I thought if I was not perfect, God would abandon me as well. However, what I learned is that nothing can separate me from the Love of God and that God was a Father to the fatherless.

As an adult I had to learn what a father daughter relationship looked like. I thought when I accepted the free gift of Jesus dying on the cross for me, things in my life would automatically change. God would give me everything I wanted. Afterall, when my natural father came around he would buy me things. I know now it was to make up for the fact that he wasn't there. Instead of God giving me things, I felt like I was being stripped of stuff. Initially, it was hard for me. I would say things to God like, I thought you were supposed to be the giver of all good things? Girl, I wanted my stuff.

Growing up with lack will make you think like that. God didn't give me what I thought I wanted. He gave me what I needed. I needed His presence and love in my life unconditionally. My relationship with God is not about things, but about His presence. Because He knows why we do the things we do, He could manage my questions, rants, and attitude.

Growing up my momma had rules, I had to follow. It was the world according to momma's household. It didn't matter what other people did in their house, she had rules established as she saw fit. I was punished if I broke her rules. I paid the penalty with a spanking. God corrects His children as well. I had to learn the chastising or discipline of the Lord was not because He was angry at me, but it was because He loved me enough not to let me continue to live my life with wrong thinking and a bad attitude. I was being stripped of wrong thoughts, attitudes, and rants because He wanted to produce peace and calm in my life. The rambling thoughts subsided as I sat in His presence. He let me get it all out. It was the residue coming to the surface. Somedays I screamed at God. Some days we laughed.

I trained my ears and mind to listen to His counsel. In healthy relationships daughters want to make their fathers proud of them. My

Heavenly Father taught me as my natural father should have. I learned to trust and love because I wanted Him pleased with me. I thought I had to be perfect for God. Girl, it's not true. He has loved me in every stage of my becoming. When I was being stubborn, He loved me. When my attitude was terrible, He loved me. When I was not my authentic self, He loved me all the more. He wanted my heart perfect towards Him.

God let me know that He loves me, and I was always accepted in Him, and He is never too busy for me. God is only a prayer or a conversation away. God will never leave me or forsake me; I am special to Him. I am not an afterthought or burden. I am not an abandoned orphan. I am His. I am His Daughter. When I hear God say Daughter, I feel His love. I have always had a Daddy. My Daddy is God.

What is Family?

I have not lived in the same state with my blood relatives in over 40 years. Most of them still only see me on social media. Girl, I had to learn that family is who you do life with. I have been "doing life "with many people, some blood relatives but mostly brothers and sisters from other mothers. My Spiritual family is as important as my natural family. Each has taught me valuable lessons in life.

I have learned what to do and what not to do from my natural and spiritual family. God had to expand my understanding of family. I do believe that God removed me from my foundational environment to expand my life views. I am not ashamed of my upbringing. It served to strengthened me. My natural foundational environment prepared me for my lifework. My spiritual family helped me to recalibrate my life on Christ, the solid foundation.

I am afforded to do life with so many sisters from other mothers. I see myself in so many women I interact with daily. I see their brokenness and pain. I empathize because I have been there. Do not let familiarity stagnate your dreams and purpose. Understand, no life experience is lost on God. He uses all our life experiences, the good, the bad, the ugly, the hurts, the pains, and the fears to strengthen us so that we can strengthened others. Girl, there is a rainbow of promises on the other side of whatever family situation you have faced. Trust God to get you to the other side.

Scripture References:

- 1 Samuel 1:1-27
- Matthew 16:13-22
- Matthew 1:1-18
- John 14:10

Girl, Be Honest With Yourself

- Have you discovered your purpose?
- If not, have you talked to God about your purpose?
- Have you had another person tease you because you lacked something that they had? It could be a child, material things, skills, economic status, or anything.
- Are you feeling like a Hannah or a Peninnah? Why?
- What walks in the room when you walk in?
- Can you say, that ain't me, to someone's perception of you?
- What are your strengths?
- What's in process in your life?
- Do you have a Teacher (truth-teller) in your life?
- Have you embraced the genuine, real you?
- Go back to the Kitchen Table Exercise and walk through the process for yourself
- What did you discover about your family dynamic?
- Do you view God through the lens of your natural father?

Girl, WHAT DO YOU NEED?

GIRL, DON'T GET STUCK

Lot's Wife
Genesis 19:26

This verse is the conclusion of the matter as it pertains to Lot's wife. She looked back and turned into a pillar of salt. This wife who is not named got stuck looking back at her past.

Years ago, I registered for a class called Introduction to Art which was a required course for the degree I pursued. My professor gave us an assignment to visit the local art museum and roam throughout the museum. I was to find something that intrigued me and write about it.

The professor wanted us to understand different expressions of art. I was bored as I walked through the museum. Baroque, Impressionism, Surrealism, blah blah, blah, and then I saw it, Art Nouveau.

I went into the children's interactive area of the museum. I saw the most fascinating thing. It was a female mannequin completely covered in jellybeans. Every inch of this mannequin was covered, even her fingertips. The vibrancy of the colors was enhanced by this shiny shellac coating on the jellybeans.

The spotlights on the ceiling served to intensify the richness of the colors of the jellybeans. It was kind of like the glistening apples in the produce section of the grocery store. The lights and the wax make the apples appear to be perfection. She was like that, fully colorful and gorgeous. However, I knew it was all lights and shadows. Someone took great care in positioning her. She was posed to look like she was walking or perhaps running.

While her body was positioned forward to look as if she was in motion walking or running, her head was in the opposite direction of her body, she was looking back at something. Behind her was a wall with a plethora of butterflies in a mosaic of brilliant colors of orange, reds, purples, greens, and blues that rival the colors of the jellybeans on the mannequin's body. Every minute or so the wings on the butterflies would flutter as if they were flying, yet they were stationary, stuck to the wall.

Like Lot's wife the mannequin was looking behind her. Lot's wife was given specific instructions to run and don't look back. You see the angels of the Lord were destroying her current dwelling place, the familiar place. They did not want her to remember that place but to focus on where she was headed, her future. But

Lot's wife looked back, and she became a pillar of salt. She became a memorial statue known only as the woman that did not embrace her future. She stayed stuck in her past. There are many lessons to learn from Lot's wife, but I will focus on her unwillingness to let go of her past mishaps, decisions, and mistakes.

I was attracted by the pretty hues of primary colors of the jellybeans on the mannequin. Upon closer examination, beneath the pretty, I saw sadness. She was stuck, forever looking backwards, never moving forward. The potential was there to go forward, but what was going on in her head made her stay focused on what was behind her. She kept looking at the butterflies stuck on the wall. Yes, they were pretty, and their wings were fluttering, but they were not flying.

Have you ever been in a place in your mind where you relive the could've, would've, should'ves of your past? We can get so stuck in replaying what we should have done that we never move forward in taking the next step. Girl, turn your head around and look towards your future. The past is in the past. It will never change no matter how much you rewrite the scenarios in your mind. Look at the past whether it be mistakes or successes as a steppingstone to the next. Becoming the real you requires you to look at past struggles as life lessons. Learn from the past, but don't get stuck.

Each day we are given 1,440 minutes. We sleep an average of 480 minutes and work an average of 480 minutes. We have 480 minutes left for everything else. Why spend those minutes regretting something you can't change? We know that each minute of the past becomes a part of our history. Look at it this way, each minute that we focus on past regrets becomes our past history. Don't let negative things in your history keep replaying over and over again in your head.

Like Lot's wife, sometimes, we like to reminisce about what happened way back when and we look up and ten years have passed. We then wonder where all the time went. Girl don't get me wrong; reflection helps you to understand how far you have come. What was it that I accomplished? What do I have to show for it? I didn't accomplish my goal because of certain situations. Life is about choices. You can choose every day to stay stuck like Lot's nameless wife or run hard towards your future.

Girl, let me tell you, the wisdom I learned so far. Days are going to be brighter. Seasons change.

People change. You can change. Keep living and keep evolving to your authentic self.

Residue in You

Girl, sometimes in your effort to move forward you must deal with the residue in you. Let me tell you about the residue in you.
As a product of a single parent home, I had many domestic responsibilities. Laundry for the household was one my responsibilities. Momma would drive me to the laundromat, unload the mountain of clothes from the car and leave me at the laundromat with washing powder, bleach, quarters, and a dime. I spent many Saturday or Sunday afternoons "doing" laundry. I had to make sure I had a dime to call Momma on the pay phone when I was finished so she could come pick me up.

I didn't mind doing laundry. It became a challenge to fold the clothes just so, so that all the clothes fitted neatly inside the laundry baskets. However, there was a chore I did not like to do, it was washing dishes. My brother and I alternated every other week with this duty. Of course, in my mind, every dish in the house was used during my week to wash. And no, we did not have the luxury of having a dishwasher. My brother and I were my momma's luxury dishwasher. Because I did not like washing dishes, I would procrastinate and wait until late in the evening to wash them. This is why it seems like every dish was used in the house. Because dishes had been sitting around all day, there would be harden food on the dishes. My solution would be to soak them overnight. Of course, that meant it was always dishes for me to clean. And Momma would get on me for leaving dishes dirty overnight.

Fast forward…I am married with children and washing dishes one day. My luxury dishwasher needed to be repaired so I found myself doing that one chore I rebelled against as a child. I was cleaning dishes and meditating on God. In my mental dialogue, I was questioning why I kept struggling with this particular area of my life.

I questioned God. I said God, if your Word is True and the Truth, why isn't it working for me?? I'm struggling. I am stuck. I continued washing the dishes and then I heard in a still quiet voice in my mind, "Is that glass clean?"

"Yes Lord, it's clean."

"Pour some water in it."

I poured the water and that's when I saw the soap. I kept rinsing and rinsing the glass, until finally the water running through the glass was clear with no soap.

God then said, "Daughter it's residue. It's the residue in you. My Word is continuously washing you."

Let's break this down: When we let dishes sit for a while, the food gook gets stuck on the dishes. What do we do? We soak the dishes. Sometimes, we have to boil water and pour the boiling water on the dishes. Heat stimulates and loosens the harden food crud.

Girl, God's Word will do the same thing. It will loosen and break up all the old gook stuck in your heart. We need to soak in His Word. That means reading and meditating on His Word consistently. Initially, it may feel like you are hurting, but it is really the fire of God's Word loosening up the residue of past struggles, errors, and choices. Don't resist, let it happen.

Here's the thing, dishes washed right after use are easier to clean than those left overnight. Have you ever scrubbed a pot left overnight and still had to pour boiling water on it to loosen the crud? You see sometimes, it takes more than one scrubbing and rinsing to be clean. That's just like our hearts, some things take more than one washing. Old wounds, old debris, old hurts, long addictive habits, take time to clean. God is merciful and loving. He will come again and again to clean up our heart. Let Him remove the residue in you.

Don't let things from your past keep you stuck. Move!

GIRL, FORGIVE TO HEAL

Tamar, Amnon, David, and Absalom
2 Samuel 13:1-34

Princess Tamar is King David's beautiful daughter. Princess Tamar wore an exquisite robe of many colors to represent her virginity. Princess Tamar had a half-brother named Amnon. Amnon lusted in his heart for his beautiful sister. He devised a plan to trap her and raped her. Princess Tamar begged him not to rape and dishonor her in that manner. She told him he could have her as a wife. She knew King David would allow it.

Amnon's lust overrode her reasoning. He not only raped her; he then told her to get out of his sight. He rejected her. Princess Tamar removed her exquisite robe of many colors and put on sack cloth and ashes. She spent the rest of her days mourning the loss of her virginity and never got married. Princess Tamar's father found out about the rape and did nothing. Her brother Absalom was outraged and waited for two years to exact revenge on Amnon. He murdered his half-brother for raping his sister Princess Tamar.

This family's tragedy has many life lessons that can be unpacked and could cover many chapters of this book, but I will focus on trauma and forgiveness.

I have many friends who like to watch Law & Order, Special Victims Unit. Hollywood spins tragic stories for entertainment and we gather faithfully week after week to watch how revenge is exacted on the perpetrators. Justice is served all neatly wrapped with a bow in just under an hour. Before there was television dramas and reality tv, there was the Bible. The Bible addresses every human experience: the good, the bad and the ugly.

In reality, those who experience trauma don't always bounce back from the experience quickly. Sometimes it is years if they ever bounce back at all. Healing from trauma starts with forgiveness.

X Marks the Spot

I took a ride with my aunt to the fish market one beautiful breezy day in California. My aunt parked on the left side of the building. This would make it easier for her to make a right turn for us to go back to the house. I stayed in the car while she went around the corner to the front entrance of the building. As I sat with the window down and was enjoying the breeze hitting my face, a woman came from the direction of the front of the building. It was clear she had picked up her fish order. She was carrying a brown paper bag and the smell of the fresh fried fish filled the air.

The lady was wearing sunglasses, yet I could tell she was staring at me. With each stride she took, she got closer to where we were parked, and I was sure she was looking at me. I glanced down, but quickly looked back up. Yes, she was for sure staring at me. The intensity of her staring through the sunglasses made me uncomfortable. She looked at me as if she knew everything about me. As she passed my car, she smirked. It was one of those side smiles people make when they smile about secret thoughts. The whole scene was surreal.

Several seconds later my aunt came from around the corner with a big smile on her face. She rushed to the car and said, "Did you see X?? You remember X?? She used to stay down the street from you all when you all stayed on ABC Street. You remember her, right?"

As, I sat in the car next to my aunt, files locked deep in my subconscious opened. It was like X's glare was the key to unlock the files. Images were racing through my mind, I needed to exhale. I was quietly suffocating under the ringing of the words, You remember X? In that moment, YES, I remembered X. She had molested me as a child. Yes, I remembered X.

The images came rushing in. My prepubescent 12-year-old self was sitting in that car watching scenes in my mind like one who sits in a theater watching a movie on the screen. I watched her take my innocence in a sadistic way. Yes, I remembered X. It was coming back to me. The images were coming too fast. I needed to breathe. Did my aunt notice I was losing my breath? I was drowning…going down for the third time. Was she going to help me? Yes, I remembered X… Breathe… Exhale… Inhale…Breathe…

"Inhale.
Exhale.
Breathe.
Girl, Whoosh!"

Reality came rushing back and I realized X had come up to the car on my side and was inviting my aunt to a party. She was too close. There was no escape. I was trapped. Silently, I screamed.

My aunt was rambling on about whether she would try to make it to the party. Lies…I knew, and she knew she wasn't going. She was just trying to be polite. X looked at me as she was talking to my aunt and said come to the party and bring her too (referring to me), we can have some fun. She knew that I knew who she was. I tensed up. My aunt missed the cue. She just laughed and said, Tojuan is only 12. That's right, I am only 12. Get away from me.

The abuse occurred sometime between the ages of 3 or 4. We relocated to another part of the city and that's when it stopped. It wasn't just sexual. It was sadistic things like trying to get me to eat a dead bird. X secretly put it between two pieces of bread and tried to get me to take a bite of her special sandwich. The images were shameful and embarrassing to think about. I wanted revenge. I hated her. I hated that she controlled me like that. My older self-wanted to jack her up. There is no doubt, I would have won the fight.

I see myself at the ages between 5-8 years, playing "doctor" with the children of my mother's boyfriend's family. On a typical Friday night, the adults would gather for Friday nights of trash talking while playing bid whist or dominoes, smoking, drinking, loud jubilant laughing, Marvin Gaye, Al Green, The Spinners, and the Whispers playing on the record player in rotation.

The adults were up front enjoying life, getting drunk and telling the kids to go play in the room. Stay out of grown folks' business they would say. The shame of our secret games made me keep quiet. We would have gotten in big trouble if they knew what we were doing. We had a couple of close calls, but never got caught.

How the Healing Began

I spent many years trying to wish away the images. I tried to drown out the images in other relationships. If I connected with someone sexually on my terms, I thought it would mend that wound in my heart. That didn't work. Girl, I don't celebrate my "body count" because for real for real, it just left another layer of shame. I wanted the pain and anger to stop.

I can look back on how my trauma left me angry. I battled with the images for many years in my mind. I hated X. I wanted revenge. I wanted her to suffer like I did. But the reality is she was probably on to the next conquests. And there I was with the images spinning around in my mind like a crib mobile on top of my head. I was one that did not tell anyone because of the shame of it. I suffered in silence because I did not know who would fight for me. I did not know who I could trust with this because I felt like it was my fault.

Where was God when this was happening? Why didn't He help me? Why didn't He punish her for what she did to me?
While all the images of X came in, so did another image. It was me. I was 3 years old. I had on a blue choir robe with a white collar. I am singing in a choir with a bunch of other children. We were singing "He's got the whole world in His hands." I see my little brown hands lifted in front of me and up to the heavens. I was singing to God. I was feeling His love all around me. Girl, to be clear, I did not grow up in church as a part of my normal ritual. Sunday mornings were sleep-in mornings. My upbringing was liberal, and church was optional. My momma said she wanted me to decide if I wanted to go to church or not. Why she felt that way is a story for another day.

God was with me all the time. He saw what happened. He shielded the full effect of it from me. I believe that's why I did not remember it for years. Surely, if He had the whole world in His hands, He had me as well. He carried me during that time. And, when the trauma was brought to the forefront of my mind, He wanted to start my healing process. However, I was more focused on revenge. He wanted me to forgive, and I wanted to fight. I did not understand the power of forgiveness. Where I come from, you don't back down from a fight. That's a sign of weakness.

Shame, that painful feeling kept arising from my consciousness and my first reaction was I wanted payback. Just like Tamar I was consumed with shame. In many ways I put on sack cloth and ashes. Whereas Tamar's shame looked more like victimization and sorrow, my sackcloth: my shame and guilt showed up as a humiliated fury. I was angry. My guilt was also present because I knew what I did with the children in the back room on Friday nights. Neither posture is authentic living.

Being continuously angry or relishing in victimhood is not healthy or authentic living. Unforgiveness and wanting revenge can lead to murder. Absalom laid in wait for two years before murdering Amnon. I know I murdered X over and over in my mind.

A victim mentality can have a person seeking sympathy over healing. The attention of people feeling sorry for them can override the need to heal. It can also be used as a crutch. I could've, would've, should've, but this happened to me. So, I am choosing to be stuck all my life. We have a choice to remain a victim or become victorious.

My victorious living started with forgiveness. Forgiveness has to do with trust and obedience. Did I want some street justice and let X catch these hands? Or did I trust God, to handle the situation?

Forgiveness does not ignore what happened to you. It acknowledges what happened but starts the process of healing and taking your power back. Girl, I had to learn that what Jesus did on the cross FOR me was greater than anything that X had done TO me. Anyone who believes in Jesus will not be ashamed. The painful things that happened in my past, could not compare to the promises God has in store for me. My life was not going to be a series of misfortunate events. My purpose was greater.

Your purpose is greater.

Forgiveness empowered me to see beyond my pain to my purpose. It was a process. There were days when I had to remind myself that I chose to forgive. The pain subsided gradually. As I focused on the One that had the whole world in His hands the pain continued to diminish. And now X marks the spot where God healed my heart.

GIRL...BREATHE!

Mary & Martha
Luke 10:38-42

The Bible speaks of Mary and Martha who were sisters. Jesus visited Martha's home, but she was consumed, running around trying to make things "nice" for Jesus. Mary, on the other hand, chose to sit and listen to Jesus as He taught. Martha got a little salty with Mary and asked Jesus to tell Mary to help her. Jesus basically told Martha to breathe and chill out. He told Martha that her sister made the right choice by sitting down and listening to Him. Mary just wanted Jesus, she was not concerned about the outward appearance of things or if the house was clean. Mary knew about hospitality and serving, but the greatest service she could do was to sit and learn from Jesus.

A Martha Mentality
John 10:10

Girl, have you ever had someone come to your home unannounced? How did it make you feel? Was your house clean? If not, were you embarrassed by the clutter? Were you running around trying to make things neat for your guest? Or did you just welcome them in?

I went through a period in my life when I had a Martha mentality. I was wearing so many hats and carrying so many suitcases that I call that time in my life the "Suitcases and Hats" phase. I was focused on getting things done and using all of my gifts. This is a partial list of some of my hats:

- Wife
- Mother
- Church Elder
- Church Chief Administrative Officer
- Tutor
- Director of a Pregnancy Resource Center
- Community Activist
- Pastoral Assistant, Friend
- Intercessor
- Grandmother
- Caterer
- Overseer of Deacons & Church Leaders
- Church Decorator

There was a suitcase for each hat. Girl, I was like an energizer bunny and the "go-to person" for everyone. I was weighed down from the tower of hats and the suitcases. I knew how to "do" church, but during this period, I was neglecting the most important thing, my alone time with Jesus. I was continuously exhausted from constantly juggling projects. My plate was not just full, things were falling off my plate. When I was running around like Martha there was no balance in my life. I was trying to be every woman with Chaka Khan and Whitney Houston singing in my ear. God does not want us to be every woman, but a specific woman with a specific purpose.

In a reference letter for employment, someone once wrote about me, "Her greatest strength is that she knows how to get things done." They added, "Her greatest weakness is that she knows how to get things done." Wow!

Like Martha, I was complaining that someone needed to help me, but I was not giving anyone the opportunity to help because I was getting it done. If any of this is familiar, say, "Ouch!"

Balancing Suitcases and Hats started affecting my health. My stress was EPIC. I went to see my family physician and she asked me a simple question, "How are you doing today?"

I opened my mouth to say the usual, "I'm fine." But I closed my eyes to inhale and exhale. When I opened my eyes a flood gate of tears erupted from the depths of my being. I managed to say, "I am tired!"

In that moment, my doctor was a safe place for me. I emptied out. I shared with her all I was doing. She told me, "Step away from all of your duties at church."

"I can't. I am too invested," I protested.

She said, "You can, and you need to do it soon."

I went home and told my husband, "My Martha mindset has to change." We knew that I needed to start putting things in place so that I could step away. My plan was to leave at the end of the year, so it would give me about 100 days or so for the transition to be smooth. A couple of days later, I shared with the leadership at church about my stress. I did not share that I was going to transition out. About a week later, my pastor called me into his office and removed me from a major assignment at church. The transition happened quickly, but I was able to unpack a major suitcase and several hats.

During this time, my husband and I went away for a weekend of prayer. I sat down on an island in the middle of a bay so that I could listen to Jesus teach me about balance. Jesus had chastised Martha for being anxious and troubled. She was busy being busy. Girl, Jesus had to remind me that I don't need to be anxious or worried. Some people referred to these happenings in life as "resets" or do overs. However, Jesus told me it was actually a recalibration not a reset. Let me explain. . .

Reset Versus Recalibration

Some people grew up eating Sunday dinner at a table. Weekly, their Momma would teach her children how to set the table to her preferences. A reset in its simplest terms is to set the table again. Resets can happen in all areas of life. Have you ever heard people say, "We need to do it like we always have done it? We need to get back to what we used to do. Remember when we did such and such?" They are saying they need to reset.

> RESET = Starting over
>
> RECALIBRATION = Moving toward a standard

When analyzing a chemical compound, a chemist compares it to an established standard and makes necessary corrections towards the standard. My husband is a chemist by profession, and he taught me that recalibration in my life is the same process. I had to reexamine my paradigm, the system of moral values, and make corrections that guided me towards God's standard. As I sat on that island, I welcomed Jesus into my unkept house. I let Him see the unclean parts while I sat at His feet and allowed Him to recalibrate me back to His standards.

I believe that Mary was seeking such a recalibration for herself. Jesus told Martha that Mary chose the one necessary thing in life…she chose Him. Recalibration and balance start with choosing Jesus. Recalibration to the Standard will help you discover who you are specifically. Recalibration will cause you to start removing hats and setting down those heavy suitcases. You will travel light in life. You will move towards the Standard of having an abundant life instead of a life of burdens. Just because you can do something does not mean you should do it.

Sometimes you have to pause and look around to see who is more equipped than you so you can share the load and celebrate the accomplishment of people who wear the hats well. Learn how to make a pivot pass like a basketball player.

Some of your hats must remain in place. For example, I am a wife, mother, and minister for God. Those three hats must be in balance in my life. I can decide how to pivot and pass the other hats. During the day, I pivot and pass, but at night, I take my hats and wig off and I breathe.

Girl, Breathe. Recalibrate.

GIRL, TRUST IN THE TRUTH

New Life
John 3:1-17

There was a girl named Vida who lived around the corner from my grandma. I used to watch her as she walked past my grandma's house on her way home from year-round school. I don't know who said hello first, but once the formalities were over, we became friends quickly. Vida was my BFF before I knew what that term meant. I was eight. She was nine.

Vida convinced my mother to enroll me in her elementary school. We were even in the same classroom when I was in 5th grade, and she was in 6th grade. We went to different junior high schools and rival high schools. The memories of staring each other down during high school football games still makes me smile. Because of attending different schools, we didn't see much of each other during those years. Whenever we did get together it was as if we had just spoken to each other the day before. Our friendship is still like that today. We live in different states, but if she calls, the day is a wash because we are going to talk for at least three or four hours. Girl, if you have any friendships like this, cherish them.

Vida and I ended up in the Washington, DC area for different reasons and reconnected in our early twenties. I was attending Howard University and Vida's fiancé was playing professional football for the Washington Redskins. When we reconnected, Vida would talk about God a lot. Neither of us attended church regularly as children so it was interesting listening to her share about her faith. I laugh now thinking about our heated conversations about Prince and if he truly was a Christian. I was a big fan of Prince, and I was not going to let anybody talk about him. Vida questioned me about my relationship with God. I always told her, "I know God is real."

She pushed further. "If you were to die today, would you go to heaven?"

Sometimes, I would think, "Is all she thinks about is God? She always wants to talk about God?"

Of course, I said, "Yes, because I am a good person."

"Being good is not your ticket to heaven."

I had no proof, but I disagreed with her. Vida asked me to watch a videotape called "Rock and

Roll: A Search for God." The video was about rock and roll musicians and how they mocked God in their music. Some had pictures of themselves hanging on crosses. Some said satan was bigger than God. It was troubling to watch. Right in the middle of all these Rock and Roll singers, was the same poster of Prince that I had hanging in my bedroom when I was in high school.

As I listened to the narrator speak about the rock singers and Prince, I realized that I was just as lost as those singers and that if I did not change my ways. I was not going to heaven like I thought, but I was going to hell. I called Vida and shared my thoughts with her.

She asked, "Do you want to be sure about getting to heaven?"

I said, "Yes." I realized that there was nothing I could do to earn my way into heaven. I asked God to forgive me for all the terrible things I did. I knew I needed a Savior. I accepted that Jesus paid the penalty for all my sin against God. He became my Savior on February 2, 1988. I had to learn to let Jesus be Lord of my life. It required me to renew my mind and thinking. I learned to live my life through the lens of the Bible, not popular opinion and I have never looked back.

GIRL, WHO IS IN YOUR TRIBE?

Ruth, Naomi and Orpah
Ruth 1:1-23

There is so much to learn from the book of Ruth: Obedience, Trusting in God in the midst of hardship, the redemptive love of Christ, marriage, and the importance of family, but I will focus on the relationship of Ruth, Naomi and Orpah. Naomi lost many things in her life. Because of a famine in her homeland, she relocated to a foreign country with her husband and her two sons. Her sons got married in the foreign land to two women named Ruth and Orpah. Time past and Naomi's husband died.

Naomi remained in the foreign land with her sons and ten years later they both died. These three women were widows. Naomi's grief was plain to see. She had heard the famine had ended in her homeland and decided to return to her native country. She urged her daughters-in-law to go back to their mother's house and she would return to her native land. They had honored her, but Naomi knew the women needed protection and basic necessities. We spoke of the patriarch society in the first chapter. If a son died, his brother would marry the wife. Naomi did not have any other sons and was too old to bear sons so the women could not remarry. At first, both women protested and said they were staying with Naomi. Naomi insisted they go back and Orpah went back to her mother's house. Ruth refused. She told Naomi, wherever you go I will go. Wherever you lodge, I will lodge. Your people shall be my people and your God shall be my God.

Girl, who will be there with you come what may? Who will see greatness and celebrate you openly and still challenge you behind closed doors? Who will get in the pit with you when you despair? Who will push you towards your purpose and not let you settle for less than your potential? Girl, who is with you? Who is your "tribe"? Who is in your circle, your ride or dies, your community, your sister friends? Your circle can determine your mobility or stagnation.

Ruth was Naomi's ride or die companion. Ruth decided no matter what was going on in Naomi's life, she was sticking by her side. She trusted Naomi. Even though Naomi was having a season of regret and feeling sorry for herself, Ruth was able to look past Naomi's moment of despair and see her for who she was, a wise woman full of wisdom. Surround yourself with people who can recognize when you are having a moment but will not let you unpack your suitcase and live in despair.

I remember a season in my life when I was just going through it. I was sitting in my church office with my head hanging low in despair. My friends surrounded me and let me cry it out, then told me to get it together. They let me have my moment but would not let me stay there, that's love.

Know this, some people are in our lives for reasons and some for seasons. Orpah loved Naomi. However, she was willing to go only so far with her. The deal breaker for Orpah was having a husband. She wanted to be married again. So, she left. It did not mean she was not loyal to Naomi during their time together. It meant her season had come to an end.

Sometimes we want to hold on to people when our purpose and destiny requires us to let them go. It doesn't mean that anything was wrong, it was just time. In our becoming we can outgrow relationships and friendships.

My circle is multi-faceted. Some in my circle are teaching me many things. Others, I am teaching. I am student and teacher in my group.

One in my circle, that has helped me to grow in many ways is Messenger Annette Carswell.

Messenger Annette Carswell

I was having trouble with a certain leader at church. The situation resulted into a very public dismantling of a project I had invested years of my life into. I was in a wounded place. The truth of the matter is I really loved the person I was striving with, she just had it in for me. I decided to sit at home and lick my wounds in private. I thought about never going to that church again.

For two weeks I sat at home crying to God about how I was being treated. It was a pity party for an audience of One. Like Naomi, I was in despair. I was so broken that if the wind had gently blown on me, I would have broken into little pieces. Like Humpty Dumpty, I probably would not have been put back together again.

One day as I was sitting in my office at home, I heard the Lord say "Get up and wash your face. Go to the church service tonight." Like my friends, He let me cry for a season and then it was time for me to get it together. I did not want to go to the church service. I knew people would be watching me. I did not want the attention.

In obedience, I got up and got dressed and dragged myself into the service. I arrived late with the plan of easing into the back row just in case I had to rush out. The door made a loud noise when I pulled it open, and all eyes were on me. Aww man, oh well…I remember many people smiling when they saw me. The guest speaker was being introduced. Her name was Messenger Annette Carswell.

The sermon is a distant blur, I just remember when she shifted and humbly shared about a time in her life when she was jealous of another lady in her church. In Messenger's eyes, this lady had it all together and she did not like her. One day she was at the pulpit and the lady came into service wearing a beautiful fur coat. She hated her for having that beautiful coat. From the pulpit, Messenger said she began to say awful things about the lady in code of course.

"Some people think they are better than others. Some people like to flaunt." Messenger said things along those lines. It was directed at the lady. She said because of her position, she could say things from the pulpit to hurt people.

No one was going to correct her because of her position in the church. With tears in her eyes, she shared how that lady never came back to her church again. She said through tears she shared about how God had to deal with her about her insecurities. Because she was hurting, she was mistreating His people. She said she asked God to forgive her and was remorseful for how she treated the woman. She prayed that the woman was still walking with God.

As I listened, I let the tears flow from my eyes unashamed. I understood well how the lady with the fur coat must have felt. For a season, it seemed as though Messenger Carswell would be in town and her sermons would speak to my current situation. Eventually, we connected on a deeper level.

Have you ever had a conversation with someone who speaks to your purpose not to your current situation? Messenger Carswell is that person for me. It was almost as if she could see who I was becoming and always spoke to my authentic self. It was as if she saw my future self and spoke to me from that stance. Although I considered her to be very mature in the things of God and wanted to glean from her insights continuously, she wanted to hear from me.

She would ask, "What is God saying to you Tee?"

At first, I was taken aback by her inquiries, but then I realized she understood the teacher student dynamic. There were things I could help her understand as well. The inquiries were also to gage the depth of my understanding of the things of God. She understands we are all connected and need each other. She is a person in my circle that has taught me many things about church order, prayer and leadership. She has challenged me to grow and step into my purpose and destiny in God.

We need people in our circle that can look beyond the obvious and speak to our destiny. Messenger Carswell is one of those people for me. Decades later Messenger Carswell continues to be that affirming Spiritual Mother, Sister, Friend, and Encourager in my life.

My circle also protects my reputation. I remember an acquaintance of my friend coming up to me and saying that my friend was protective of me. Apparently, someone said something about me that was negative. My friend defended my reputation. My sister friend was not letting anyone come for me. Have people in your circle that speak well of you when you are not around.

Girl, I grew up with the mindset that I could address issues with my friends privately...we could shout it out, if necessary, but in public we were united. The circle encourages. The circle protects and covers you. The circle teaches you. You teach in the circle. The circle loves you. You love in the circle. The circle is a continuous bond.

Scripture References:

- Genesis 19:26
- 2 Samuel 13:1-34
- Luke 10:38-42
- John 10:10
- John 3:1-17
- Ruth 1:1-23

Girl, Be Honest With Yourself

- Do you feel stuck right now? Why?
- How do you identify the residue you?
- How do you process your past successes or mistakes?
- Can you trust God to wash it away? Why or why not?
- Do you have some unresolved trauma? Can you trust God to heal it?
- What does starting the process of forgiveness look like for you? Talking to God? Therapy?
- Is there anyone you can trust with your story? Who is your Ruth? Who is with you no matter what?
- Make a list of the hats you wear and the suitcases you carry. Are they weighing you down? Can you pivot and pass something to others?
- Are you resetting or recalibrating?
- Describe a time in your life when your season shifted, and you needed to move forward.
- Who or what in your life is hindering your greatness and why?

Girl, WHAT IS LOVE?

GIRL, SEX IS A GIFT

Wisdom Speaks
Titus 2: 3-5

This scripture is speaking to women helping or instructing women, specifically older or mature women helping younger women navigate through life. I believe women of all ages need mentoring in various areas of life. We need women of wisdom to point us towards the direction of success. I spent years letting experience teach me things. I know now that wisdom could have saved me a lot of pain in my life. In some situations, I should have listened to sound advice.

If you have read this book thus far, you know I made many mistakes and learned many things along the way. I don't share these things because I have arrived, and you need to listen to me. I share these things because I am still becoming and want to share the knowledge obtained on my journey to becoming.

Can We Talk?

I heard it said that knowledge is power. I think this is a half-truth. Application of knowledge is power. It is not enough to know a thing; you must apply what you know. The Bible says faith without works is dead. In other words, if you believe that God is doing a certain thing in your life, your actions should reflect your beliefs.

Opening Gifts

When I was a child, I played jacks in the living room. My ball went under the couch. As I got on my belly and looked under the couch to retrieve my ball, I saw them. I discovered Momma had hidden gifts behind the couch. My curiosity got the best of me. I wanted to know what was behind the pretty wrapping paper. I carefully unwrapped the gifts to see what was inside. I remember being excited about some of the gifts I saw and then I rewrapped the gifts.

On Christmas morning, when I was handed my gifts, I had to pretend like I had not seen the gifts. The elation for the gifts were not there anymore. I opened the gift before it was time and now there was no special excitement in me. I was faking.

In many ways sex is the same way. The Bible says do not awaken love before it's time. Some things need to stay asleep until the right moment for them to be awaken. This is how God designed sex. It is the gift that a husband and wife are supposed to open together and celebrate together. Trouble arises when the gift is open too early. Sometimes, it is opened by the wrong person. Those gifts behind the couch…they were not all mine. I had opened other people's things.

Guard Your Heart

This is the conversation we need to be having about sex and virginity. Ahhh virginity…the taboo word of the times. Society has villainized this sacred word. Girl, I wish someone had shared with me the preciousness of virginity. How valuable a gift it is to give that one time. If I had been told that I would find someone worthy of ransoming my heart, someone worthy of my precious gift, I probably would have waited to open it.

If I had known, I would have treasured my virginity more. Society says it's just sex. It is just physically making each other feel good. I remember a girl saying that to me.

I point blank asked her had she ever had an orgasm? (There is a boldness that comes over me sometimes!) She had not. So, I said, it seems like you are giving of yourself to make *him* feel good. Girl, you are not an animal in heat! Girlllll!!!!!

Sex is SPIRITUAL! Your whole being is engaged, body, soul, and spirit. You are receiving and giving a part of yourself to the other person and that person is giving a part of himself to you. Issues arise when you are giving yourself to so many people. You become fragmented and pieces of you are spread everywhere. Don't let society tell you it is *just an act* because it is not.

The Business of Sex

Sex sales. Sex is a money maker in our society. It is a trillion-dollar industry that crosses all spectrums of daily living. Sex is everywhere, media (reality tv, dramas, comedies, cartoons, and movies), music (lyrics and videos), magazines (images, BBL, breast implants, Botox, fashion of partially dressed men and women), schools (children's picture books, free condoms, and birth control pill distribution) games (toys, plastic and "living" dolls, video games) and technology (pornography with a click of a button, sexting) to name a few.

Society has degraded the beauty of God's intent for sexual intimacy with lewd images and actions. There is a celebration of sexual freedom. Rarely are consequences of our sexual freedom discussed. Rarely are women told condoms cannot protect your heart. Women are singing about W.A.P.'s and teaching the next generation as well. There was a time when we wanted a ring on our finger. Now, we just want a cuffing season. We dance to beats and do not pay attention to the lyrics. We twerk at every turn.

We teach men to devalue us with our actions. We are half-naked out here trying to attract Delaquan and not realizing his slimy uncle JJ and stud auntie DD are watching you as well. We have lost modesty and femininity. Some things do not need to be on display for all to see. Society says just do it if it makes you feel good. YOLO - You only live once.

The consequences of impulsive actions can last a lifetime. This daredevil, Russian roulette, unaware, it could never happen to me mindset comes into my center weekly. It is then I am allowed to have the conversation, we should be having with all women.

How to Put Love Back to Sleep

It is possible to abstain from sex once who have started. Remember just because you can do something, doesn't mean that you should. Starve the urges. It will require changes in behavior, environments, and relationships. Remember when I said that experience brought pain in my life that wisdom could have prevented. Wisdom could have prevented my heart from being wounded and my body being used.

Change sometimes requires an accountability partner. When changing a habit, your body has to unlearn what it has been accustomed to having. The flesh goes through withdraws because it wants what it wants. When it is sexual withdrawal, your body can feel like it's on fire. Resist! Call somebody who can talk you pass the urges. Other things to consider:

- *Pray and ask God to help you* – Trust the process.
- *Guard your thoughts* – This may require you to change what you read and focus your mind on. The Bible says to think on things that are true, noble, just, pure, lovely and of a good report.
- *Guard your eyes* – Monitor what you watch on media outlets and technology. During my season of withdrawal, I would turn the magazines backwards in the stores. I did not want to look at subtle suggestive pictures while waiting in line at the grocery store.
- *Guard your ears* – A lot of music that is being produce is basically sex talk without consequences. No 2:00 am booty call conversations.

- *Guard your relationships* – Hang out with groups of friends or people. Join organizations or groups that have group activities or outings. I have friends that are part of painting groups, travel groups and things of that nature. Remember when I said He who finds a wife find a good thing. It does not say he who finds a girlfriend, side chick, booty call, cougar, or sugar momma. Do not let anyone devalue your worth.

It has been said that to change a habit or behavior, it takes 30 days to unlearn a habit, 30 days to relearn a new habit and another 30 days for the new habit to become a routine. Your process may be 90 days or longer, but you can do it with help from your accountability partner and God.

GIRL, IS MARRIAGE FOR YOU?

Adam and Eve
Genesis 2: 20 -25

The wedding ceremony of Adam and Eve was simple. God saw that Adam was alone. The animals had mates, but Adam did not. God made Adam from the dust of the earth. But Eve was special. He fashioned her from the rib of Adam. God presented Eve to Adam. He looked at her and knew she was his. She was his woman (womb-man) because she came out of him. They were naked and not ashamed.

Many women dream about their special day. They imagine the beautiful dress with the long train and the fragrance of flowers saturating the atmosphere with sweetness. The violins, the exchanging of rings, the food, the laughter, and merriment, the first dance…the romance. Love is in the air. The bride is her most beautiful. The groom is fresh and debonair. The bride and groom sneak loving glances at each other all night. The guests requesting kisses by chiming the wine glasses with their silverware. The cutting of the cake, the throwing of the bouquet to all the single ladies, because the bride is married now. The wonderment in their eyes says, Love, love will keep us together. I am a hopeless romantic. I love weddings. However, a perfect wedding day does not equate to a perfect marriage. A wedding happens on one day or more depending on your culture. A marriage is supposed to last until death of the spouse.

> *He who finds a wife finds a good thing and obtains favor from the LORD.*
>
> Proverbs 18:22

I remember writing a paper in college about love. I wrote love is long walks in the park on a beautiful spring day. Love is flowers, chocolates, and candle lit dinners. Love is getting the oil in my car changed. You see there is a practical side to love and marriage that can get lost in the midst of all the romance. Marriage can be full of romance and love, but it is naïve to think once you get married every day is going to be a fairytale. For real for real, there have been days when my husband and I did not like each other at all. Girl, I have learned that love is a decision I make every day. A successful marriage requires 100% effort from both spouses. Marriage is not about two people giving fifty-fifty to make a whole.

> **Think about these equations...**
>
> $\frac{1}{2} \times \frac{1}{2} = \frac{1}{4}$
>
> $1 \times 1 = 1$

Both must be all in for the marriage to thrive and survive the cares of life: finances (Girllll!), intimacy (Girlll!), communication (can we talk?) and family (Woosah!). Marriage is compromise. Marriage is service one to another. Marriage is sacrifice. Marriage is acceptance of each other, flaws, and all. Marriage is esteeming the others needs above your own. Marriage is encouraging each other to be the best version of his or herself. Marriage is not always easy, but it is worth it. Marriage is work, but marriage works. Ask yourself, is marriage for you?

Marriage was God's idea from the start, so it is necessary for a Him to be a part of it for it to be successful.

God wants a man and woman to become one. The man is charged to leave his mother and father and cleave to his wife. That means no one should come between the unity of the husband and wife, not even their parents and family members. Problems can arise when this is not established and understood because everybody has an opinion. This does not mean parents cannot give sound advice to the couple. Parental wisdom can be beneficial to the couple. But the couple's parents must recognize the uniqueness of the couple, because each and every marriage is different. There is Tojuan, the unique person and there is Donald, the unique person.

The oneness that is DonaldTojuan or DonJuan as we call ourselves is separate from the children our parents raised. The DonJuan entity along with God in the midst is the most important relationship in my life. And while we are here…children should not come before your spouse. The order that God has established is God, husband, wife, children and then everything else. When it is not in this order, problems arise. Is marriage for you?

Financial struggles can cause strain on marriages more than anything. I learned to appreciate my husband's strength in our struggles. He sacrificed for our family. He worked several jobs so I could be home with our children. He never said I had to work. It has always been my choice to work because he is responsible for us. We have been in lack as well as abundance. My children told me they figured out what I was doing in the early lean days. Dinner was basically ground turkey, pasta, and a sauce.

Depending on the noodle, I would give the dish a different name. They told me you basically made spaghetti almost every day. HAHAHA! It's true. They ate spaghetti, fettuccini casserole, ziti bake, spaghetti bake, lasagna baked, and many others and it was all pasta, meat, sauce, and a little twist to make it unique.

Intimacy is important in marriage. God created sex. We discussed it earlier. It is for procreation, recreation, and relaxation. Depending on what stage you are at in life, one of the forms of intimacy will dominate. Sometimes several forms at the same time can come into play. Sex should not be laborious, but a celebration of the union of husband and wife. If this is not the case for you, seek a safe person who can help you in this area. Sexual intimacy was supposed to be reserve as a gift between husband and wife after they were married. They were to be naked and not ashamed. Problems can arise when one or both spouses compare previous intimate encounters to their current relationship.

Are You the Good Thing?

The Bible speaks of when a man finds a wife, he finds a good thing and obtains favor from the Lord. Girl, are You the good thing that is lacking in his life?

I was sitting in the lobby of Carver Hall at Howard University. It was February 1985. My two friends had convinced me to go to the 25 cents dance at Carver Hall. When we arrived and went to the basement for the dance, we found there was no one there. I guess the real party was happening elsewhere because you could hear crickets on the dance floor. We came back upstairs and were discussing what to do next.

I was frustrated because I really didn't want to come, and my friends convinced me I would have a good time. I looked cute too! I was deflated. We started talking about leaving and going to McDonald's to get an apple pie to share. I was sitting with my head down and I heard someone say, "Would any of you ladies like to dance?" I jumped up and said I would. I started walking towards the basement make-shift dance floor. It wasn't until I was walking onto the dance floor that I turned and looked at him. I said, "Hi, my name is Tojuan." He said, "My name is Donald." He smiled and the light reflecting off his braces lit the dark dingy dance floor. It was like he had a halo around his head. There was brightness all around him. I instantly liked his braces. Weird, huh? Two other guys started dancing with my friends and the six of us were the party. I soon discovered he had one dance move, the sidestep.

We danced together for hours. The dance turned into a serious spades game. We all went to Donald's room to get the cards. That's when I discovered his two younger sisters were sleep in his room and visiting him for the weekend. We all ended the evening going to Giant Food on P Street and buying Eggo waffles and syrup. We toasted Eggo's in somebody's dorm which was a violation of the dorm rules and we all left. Thirty years later, when we renewed our marriage vows, we had a chicken and waffle bar to honor our first meal together. I love romance and weddings.

We spent almost every day after that night together. He was a Chemistry major, and he tutored me in Chemistry. He is cerebral. I am zany. He said he liked my passion for things that were important to me. I relished his calm.

People thought we were an unusual couple, but really, he is my calm side, and I am his zany side. I can be quiet at times, and he can be the life of the party at times. We are two imperfect people that are perfect for each other. Donald found me, his good thing. After about a month, I knew I would marry him. We didn't get married until a year and a have later. We laugh with our children that he never proposed to me. One day we were sitting around, and I said, we're gonna get married huh? He said, "Yes."

I said, "I know." There was no romantic dinner or surprise video. We just knew.

Just because we knew, did not mean we did not have challenges in our marriage. I did not have a pattern before me on what a healthy marriage looked like. After all, my mother fled her violent marriage. My grandmother, although married ,appeared to had got married because she was pregnant. Almost all my aunts and uncles were single mothers or fathers, so the fact that I even got married was not the norm in my family. My husband grew up with his mother, father, and siblings. His parents were married for over fifty years.

Early in our marriage because I lacked a healthy pattern, I compared our marriage to those I felt were successful. I would watch other couples and wonder why my husband did not act like the other husbands. They seemed strong and confident in what they wanted. Not that my husband is not strong, because he is, but he would always ask me what I wanted to do. I thought he was being indecisive because he would answer my question with a question. I wanted him to just say what he wanted. I remember praying and talking to God about it.

I questioned why Donald could never seem to "make a decision" alone. I had a little attitude in my prayer that morning. Well, God sure enough did burst the high and mighty bubble that I was on that day. He said Donald makes decisions every day. Donald has decided to lay down his life for you. Donald has decided to love you as Christ loved the church. Christ gave His life for the church. Your husband gives his life for you. He loves you so much he wants to consider your needs first when "making a decision." WOW! Quickly, I dropped to my knees before God. Actually, I laid prostrate on the floor. I cried out for forgiveness. I repented for my mistaken thinking.

Sacrificial, unconditional love was always present, and I did not recognize it. I did not know how to receive it. How naïve of me. How unaware of me. I did not recognize that kind of love, because I had never seen it patterned before me. God showed me this is how we are to be for each other. I think my mindset stemmed from watching the women in my family have to make all the decisions alone. So, when Donald would asked me what I wanted to do, part of me on the inside would scream, "Why do I have to do all the decision making?"

Donald was patient with me and my attitude. The reality is I did not know what I wanted to do. I was still becoming. Girl, being married did not mean I had arrived at the height of womanhood. It was really the start of God reshaping me. God has taught me so many things about myself through the covenant of marriage. My attitude, my bad habits, my fierce independence were character traits that God reshaped for His glory. I needed a man who would patiently love me as God peeled the layers off of me. Is marriage for you?

Don-Juan

I met my husband Donald at a dance. We continue to dance together. I liken us to ballroom dancers. In ballroom dancing the man holds the frame. He is the strength. The man places his hand in the curve of the females back. He applies gentle pressure on her back. The pressure determines the direction in which way they are going to move across the dance floor. He leads. She elegantly follows.

They move as a unit. Neither tries to outshine or out dance the other. They must be synchronized in the movements and expressions. The stability of the man's frame allows the woman to move freely as she does the fancy twirls and moves. Donald frames me well and has allowed me to twirl and dance all over the place. When there is a need for me to get focused, like the dancer he gently applies pressure to my back so that we are in synch with each other and back in proper frame.

Every day we make the decision to commit to love. Donald can do this because he first loves God. His love for God makes him love me. It is the same for me. God is first. My love for God makes me honor and love Donald. That doesn't mean we do not disagree. We have learned to set parameters when we are having heated discussions. I am passionate in my expressions, so the parameters are necessary. We do not use absolutes. He doesn't always do things I don't like and vice versa. After all these years, when we are disagreeing, I must first consider if he is tired or hangry. If so, I know it's hunger talk. I extend grace. Donald does the same for me. Disagreements can be squashed with food and sleep. LOL! The key to our success is no matter what, when we retire to bed, we reach out for each other.

GIRL, SOMEBODY IS WATCHING

I saw a video of young child of about 4 years old cussing up a storm. The adults that were filming her were laughing because they thought it was cute. My heart ached as I watched. I wondered if her mother was going to find it amusing when the girl started cussing her out. Children watch the actions of their parents and do as their parents do. That old saying do as I say not as I do is wacky. It teaches our children to distrust us because we are not being authentic. If they see you cuss, they will cuss. If they see you get high, they will want to experiment with it. If they see you being promiscuous, they will follow suit.

One of the goals of our marriage was to pattern a stable, healthy relationship before our children. It was important to me that my children had a foundation that was different from mine. Girl, we didn't always get everything right, but we knew how to humble ourselves before God and our children when we were in error.

Modern Day Courtship

She was having so much fun at the local amusement center and she ran right in front of me. Our families were members of the same church. I had invited her family to join our family for a private event my job was hosting. She was playing by the putt golf course, and I remember I said in my mind, look at Courtney. Look at Kevin's wife. I was shocked by that thought, but I knew God had let me in on a secret. She was around eleven years old at the time. I just smiled as she played. I didn't say anything to my son or her. As the years passed, Kevin knew I knew who his wife would be, but I never said her name.

When Kevin was about fifteen or sixteen is when he really saw her. Remember, he who finds a wife finds a good thing… He wanted to ask her to a dance but was a little nervous. I counselled him and said if you really want to go to the dance with her, call her father and ask him for his permission to speak to her. My goal was to set a biblical foundation for courtship for them. I wanted him to show respect for her father's position in her life. You don't just call her; you ask the chief man in her life for permission.

This was not about him trying to get a girlfriend and a date to the dance. He called her father and asked permission to call her. Her father agreed, but he said it was her decision if wanted to go to the dance or not. He got up the nerve to call her and ask her to the dance. She said no. Kevin was devastated. He was crushed. He said she doesn't like me. I told him she did not reject him; she rejected the dance. Months went by and they would speak at church. I remember one day we arrived a church and there was an empty seat next to Courtney. I looked at him and said something like go sit by her and get to know her. He sat by her, and she did not look disgusted by his action.

Months went by and he wanted to ask her to the prom. I told him to call her father again and ask permission to call her. He did and got permission. He worked himself into a tizzy before calling her. He just knew she would reject him again. He went back and forth for several weeks. I had had enough of his hesitating and literally threatened bodily harm if he did not call her that night. She said yes. He was a senior in high school. She was a junior. They went to dinner and then went to the prom for 5 minutes and left. (Did not take pictures first) They left prom, went and bought socks from the dollar store and went bowling. From that day on they were always together. Their courtship was sweet.

Kevin told me her father asked him what his intentions with his daughter were. He told her father; she will be my wife. I never looked at her as a girlfriend. When she leaves your house, I will take care of her. She will not come home crying to you. After Courtney graduated high school, they met with us and her parents and told us they planned to get married. They laid out their plan on how they were to support themselves and where they were going to live. They wanted our blessings, but they planned on getting married in 4 months or so. We parents had one request. We felt they should have pre-marital counseling.

They agreed but would not counsel with us. We asked a mature couple in our church to counsel them. The couple reported back to us that they would be fine. They did get married several months later. She was nineteen and he was twenty-one. We later found out that many people thought they were getting married so young because they thought Courtney was pregnant. She was not. They were married seven years before they had a child. They wanted to be with each other. That was fourteen years ago. Kevin has kept his word to take care of Courtney. She worked because she wanted to, not because she had to work. She stays home with their daughters and takes care of Kevin.

I told Kevin I knew she would be his wife after he knew she was the one. Parents sometimes know who is best for their children. Courtney and Kevin are two young people who had a pattern of covenant married relationship to observe. Courtney's parents have been married for over 30 years. We could offer them sound counsel when things were challenging for them. One of the greatest things my daughter in love said to me was thank you for my Kevin.

Let me put this right here, Girl, let him pursue you. Men love a challenge. Men also recognize women who are desperate for attention. The desperados they will seduce with flowering words to fulfill their ultimate goal of having sex with you. You see men are attracted by what they see, and women are attracted by what they hear. Women lose when they give in to temptation. When a woman knows her worth, she will protect her heart from the smooth talkers.

Remember, you are the good thing.

Scripture References:

- Titus 2: 3-5
- Genesis 2: 20 -25
- Proverbs 18:22

Girl, Be Honest With Yourself

- Has your love awakened too soon?
- Do you want to put it back to sleep? Do you have an accountability partner?
- Are you considering all your options/choices for healthy living?
- Did you have a healthy pattern of marriage in your upbringing?
- Do you want to be married?
- If yes, why? If not, why?
- What patterns are you modeling for people to see?
- Is he is pursuing you, are you pursuing him?
- Do you know your worth?

Conclusion

GIRL, YOU ARE STRONG

Hey Girl,

It's been said that a rose by any other name is still a rose. My goal for this book was to teach you how to look deep into yourself and not be repelled by what you see.

These pages are filled with my fears, mistakes, and dreams. It is my hope that you will see yourself in these pages and reach beyond where you are in order to press towards your purpose. Stop going through the motions that are not making progress and take a step toward your true identity in God.

Continue to ponder the questions that I asked. Get with a sister circle at church, with friends, in your family, or at work and dig deeper. Do not be ashamed of where you are, you are growing. I want this for you because I want you healed, strong and I want you settled in your identity.

I gave you everything that I did not have growing into my womanhood. I knew that there was more to life than what I was experiencing. I want the fullness of everything God has promised me. When others saw a glimpse of my purpose and destiny, I had to learn how to receive their wisdom. Now that I am a mature woman, I have a responsibility to you, because I see you. I myself in you.

Just like the rose by any other name is still a rose, you are God's child. He was concerned about how He defined you when He knew you before you were formed in your mother's womb. God has great plans in store you. Girl, Come Forth.

I love you,

Tojuan